2008

Poetry and Stories

by
6th grade students of
Fairfield Middle School

1st WORLD
LIBRARY
Literary Society

2008

Poetry and Stories

by 6th grade students of Fairfield Middle School

© 1st World Library - Literary Society, 2009
P. O. Box 2211, Fairfield, Iowa 52556
• Tel: 641-209-5000 • Fax: 641-209-3001
• Web: www.1stworldlibrary.com

First Edition

LCCN: 2009922804

SoftCover ISBN: 978-1-4218-9069-2
HardCover ISBN: 978-1-4218-9068-5
eBook ISBN: 978-1-4218-9070-8

Foreword

I write to discover my soul; I read to discover yours.

Why is a publication of student writing worthy of awe and celebration? It is worthy of such response because of the miracle it represents. When students engage in writing, everything becomes more than it seems. Writers become more than students in seats. Poetry becomes more than an assignment. Teachers become more than knowledge keepers. Discovery becomes the way of life. This compilation of student writing represents an FMS habit of becoming "more." Student writing is beautiful not because of its form or its structure, but rather because of its representation of individuality and thought. When students write, they begin the process of discovering their souls. Writers take a risks when the compose thoughts that represent how they process the world in which they live and solidify their place in it. At the same time, the reader also takes a risk to embrace an opportunity to make meaning in their own lives. This reciprocal meaning cements a relationship between reader and writer that cannot be defined or fragmented. Many times, in the classroom, student success is dependent upon ability to arrange external information in clear and concise forms. We all know that life is rarely clear and concise and the most effective method for relaying our interpretation of it typically rests within ourselves,

1

not someone else. Transformations abound beyond the cover of this book. Words become passages to understanding for everyone involved. To the student writers of Fairfield Middle School, thank you for this opportunity to look at my own precious life. The beauty of your words inspires all.

Marci Dunlap,
Director of Curriculum
Fairfield Community School District

Introduction

The poems and stories you are about to read were written and selected by sixth graders of the Fairfield Middle School in Iowa. These eleven- and twelve-year-olds were exposed to a wide variety of writing throughout the year. During our Poetry Unit, students read, chanted, sang, acted-out, interpreted, memorized, and recited poems from famous authors. They also learned how to write many different types of poems, including Japanese tanka, haiku and magazine haiku, acrostic, bio, cinquain, color poems, concrete, couplets, diamanté, holiday poems, limericks, ocean research, and title down poems. The poems in this book are the culmination of what they learned. Some are funny, clever, creative, and silly, while others are serious or sad; yet all convey the thoughts and emotions of these young, budding writers. The stories in this book were sometimes inspired by a story prompt, or from a journal entry; but mainly they come from their creative imaginations. I'm proud of their work and willingness to share this personal side of themselves with others. Happy reading!

Ann Gookin,
6th Grade Language Arts Teacher
Fairfield Middle School

Haiku (hi'koo) Poetry

A traditional Japanese verse, written in 17 syllables
divided into three unrhymed lines made up of
five, seven, and five syllables, often on the
subject of nature or the seasons.

Haiku

Floating through the air
Bright colors lacing darkness
Silky wings on skin

Henry Armbruster

Rainbow

Staying in the sky
Red, yellow, orange, blue, lime green,
Coming after rain

Krystal Weirup

The River

Water rushing past,
Birds singing a merry tune,
I sit peacefully.

Rachel Biggs

Shoes, Shoes!

Shoes, shoes, too many
To choose. Red, green, and purple,
Too many to choose!

Danielle Cassiday

Magazine Haiku (hi'koo) Poetry

We put a spin on the traditional Japanese verse by
adding inspirational pictures from magazines
and using them as our subject.

Magazine Haiku

The cool flying V
It's a wonderful guitar
And the sound is great.

Jake McLain

Shelby Mustang GT 500

Red Shelby Mustang
Inventor Carroll Shelby
I am related

Austin Shelby

Color Poetry

A poem written about a favorite color,
using the five senses:

Taste, touch, smell, sight and sound.

This poem is packed with imagery and metaphor.

Black

Black is Goth and pain and cold.
Black is the taste of burnt toast.
Morbidness makes me feel black.
Black is the sound of nothing and shattering glass.
Black is the night sky, a burned out star,
and being lost.
Crashing is black.
Black is smoke in the night.

Fallyn Garrison

Orange

Orange is a basketball and a goldfish
And soft like a baby's skin.
Orange is the taste of a clementine.
Energy makes me feel orange.
Orange is the sound of giggles and a flute.
Orange is a sunset, jumping in leaves,
And a Trojan basketball game.
A sleepover with close friends is orange.
Orange is the smell of a tropical perfume.

Halie Meador

Passion Pink

Passion pink is strawberries and the occasional rose
And a happiness that never fades.
Passion pink is the taste of sweet cherries fully
ripened.
Sharing a smile with someone in need
Makes me feel passion pink.
Passion pink is the sound of laughter
And birds in the early morning.
Passion pink is a dance studio full of dancers
Dancing their best, a field full of flowers in full
bloom,
And the sky just after sunrise.
Living the life you dreamed of is passion pink.
Passion pink is your heart.

Makayla Kessel

19

Gold

Gold is gold pieces & bananas,
Cold & smooth.
Gold is the taste of muffins.
Winning the Olympics makes me feel gold.
Gold is the sound of French horns & tubas.
Gold is England, Israel, & libraries.
Counting money makes me feel gold.
Gold is sharp cheddar cheese.

Ian Stakland

Sky Blue

Sky blue is the ocean and bluebell flowers
And silky smooth.
Sky blue is the taste of sour blueberry slushies.
Laughing with friends makes me feel sky blue.
Sky blue is the sound of birds chirping
And people laughing.
Sky blue is a big city, my room, and the beach.
Sky diving is sky blue.
Sky blue is fresh air.

Valerie Payne

Pink

Pink is watermelon and pink tulips
And soft like a baby pig.
Pink is the taste of strawberry ice cream.
Being in front of people by myself makes
me feel pink.
Pink is the sound of hearts beating
And people laughing.
Pink is a store, a farm with pigs,
My grandparent's house with all my family.
Pink is the smell of bubble gum.

Krystal Weirup

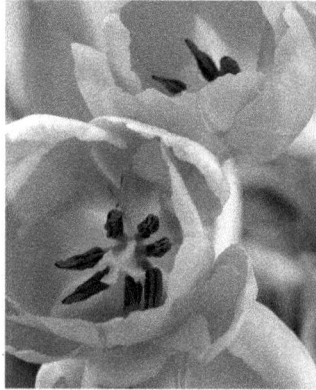

Diamanté
(dee-*uh*-mahn-**tey**)Poetry

Diamante is a form of unrhymed poetry,
made up of 7 lines, the shape of a diamond. It begins
and ends with nouns of opposite meaning, and is written as a
comparison. Lines 2 and 6 use adjectives to describe the nouns,
and lines 3 and 5 use action verbs. The middle line 4 is the
magical line, where the subject gradually transforms
from one meaning to another.

Huma
Elegant, proper
Dancing, running, jogging
California, lifeguard, *Illinois, babysitter*
Teasing, jumping, bowling
Evil, sarcastic
Brooke

Brooke Stever

P-47 Thunderbolt
Durable, tough
Shooting, maneuvering, dog-fighting
Propeller, guns, blade, rudder,
Shooting, turning, swerving,
Slow, guns
Black hawk helicopters

Austin Francisco

Duck
Yellow, soft
Quacking, waddling, flying
Feathers, web-feet, curly tail, swine
Oinking, rolling, chomping
Smelly, filthy
Pig

Cheyanne Laux

Goth
Black, red
Cutting, burning, piercing
Satan, drugs, awards, A's
Leading, cheering, smiling
Happy, bright
Preppy

Fallyn Garrison

Summer
Hot, light
Swimming, running, soccer-playing
Water, waves, snow, wind
Sledding, reading, cocoa-drinking
Cold, icy
Winter

Huma Liptak

Girls
Pretty, nice
Helping, laughing, singing
Dance, ponytails, *baseball, bugs*
Pushing, hurting, hitting
Mean, weird
Boys

Jaclyn Flinspach

Swimming
Wet, warm
Diving, pulling, flip-turning
Swim caps, swim suits, ball, jerseys
Running, shooting, free-throwing
Hot, sweaty
Basketball

Kara Greiner

Soccer
Defense, offense
Kicking, crossing, passing
David Beckham, goalie, *pitcher, catcher*
Batting, catching, throwing,
Infield, outfield
Softball

Keri Schwarz

Cat
Furry, cute
Prowling, cuddling, purring
Lap, pet, pond, lily pad
Hopping, swimming, chirping
Slimy, green
Frog

McKenna Ledger

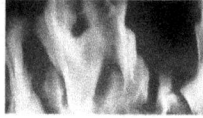

Fire
Hot, curious
Dancing, jumping, spreading
Embers, wood, diamonds, water
Sitting, hanging, melting
Cold, still
Ice

Nick Rich

Sun
Bright, yellow
Swimming, biking, playing
Park, pool, stars, bedroom
Sleeping, snoring, resting
Dark, quiet
Moon

Valerie Payne

Title Down Poetry

A poem that vertically tells a story,
using the letters of its title.

Baseball

Brand new bats
Are waiting to be
Swung,
Eighteen
Ball games
Are played in our
Little
League for fun

Jordan Whitney

Sheep

Silly farm animals
Help
Each other
Escape from the
Pen every day

Ethan Tillis

Baseball

Batting is so
Awesome,
Shaking it off,
Effort, effort, effort,
Backing up in the field,
All the hard work,
Legging it out to first,
Longing for a win.

Keith Burns

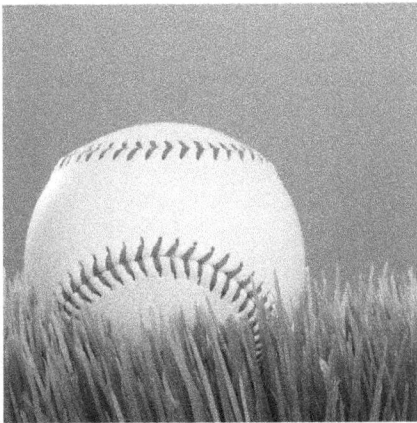

Love/Hate

Horror of life,
A lover gone.
The pity of the
End.

Lo〉ve

Keith Burns

Acrostic (*uh*-kraw'-stik) Poetry

A short poem in which the initial letters of the lines, taken in order, spell a person's name.

Vincent Horras

Victorious
Invincible
Nincompoop
Charming
Entertaining
Neat
Tidy

Huge
Original
Ripped
Rocket-fast
Active
Smart

Vincent Horras

Tanka (täng'*kuh*) Poetry

A Japanese poem consisting of 31 syllables in 5 lines, with 5 syllables in the first and third lines, and 7 in the others.

The Practice Round

I go to the course
To practice and practice well
Too hot to handle
I got my share of birdies
Wow, I shot in the 30's!

Alex Shier

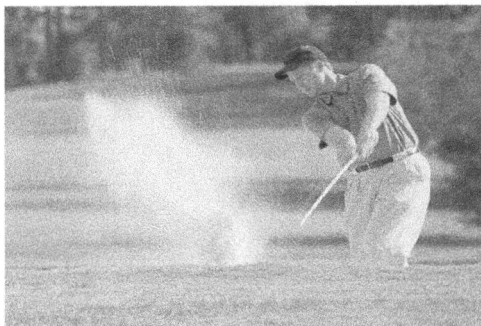

The Delicate Leaf

The delicate leaf
Hangs by but a thread of green
It sways in the wind
Hoping that it will not fall,
But be carried by the breeze.

Brooke Stever

Home Run

Run around the bags,
Round first, second, third, and home,
Over the tall fence,
Making the score go higher,
Everybody cheers for you!

Chet Vogt

Puppy

Watch that dog waiting
Waiting for her to come home
As he wags his tail
The door starts to open up
He runs happily to her.

Claudia Sloat

Ducks

Colorful and fat
Always swimming happily
Eating all the plants
Being hunted by people
Tastes really good on my plate.

Colby Jones

Fall

Leaves changing colors,
Leaves falling from the treetops,
Hanging out with friends,
Staying up late with best friends,
After fall goes, winter comes

Erica Winslow

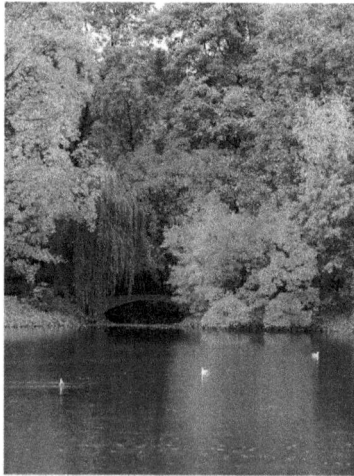

Monster Infielder

Covering the base
Running, diving for the ball
How fast can you be?
Run to the sound of the beat
Charge the ball that I can beat.

Erica Topping

Roller Coasters

Curving and swerving,
Going so extremely fast,
Climbing up so high,
Down it goes, everyone screams,
Ride is over, I feel sick.

Joanna Funkhouser

Skateboarding

I skate everywhere
I've been stopped by the police
I've fallen off stairs
So wear a helmet, it's safe
And please, oh please, try to skate.

Jonah Dowell

Very Odd Mascots

Jumping up and down,
Dancing like they lost their head
Looking so silly
And so very hideous,
Just like that one named Herky.

Joseph Hietpas

Summer

Swimming so much fun
Tanning, singing, having fun
The sun in my eyes
Cute lifeguards and puppy dogs
Sleepovers that never end.

Kara Greiner

Best Friends

Always together,
Laughing and acting stupid,
Inseparable
Since we first met very long
Ago, when we were so young.

Lalita Martin

Golf

Blue, clear, cloudless sky,
Tiger lining up his shot,
Crush it to the green,
Five feet within the round cup,
Sink the putt to win the match.

Landon Gamrath

Bunny Rabbits

Furry, small, evil
Prancing around happily,
Vegetarians
Prey of fox, snake, wolf, and bears,
Not good pets, so don't try it!

Laura Jackson

Always

Raindrops fall on me,
Golden sunrays shine on me,
Moonbeams touch my skin,
Colorful leaves brush my hair,
I am the Earthen Woman.

Leanna Miller

Demons

Ripping and shredding
Their claws are as strong as steel
They hate living things
They have no soul for kindness
They are mostly red and black.

Matt Juarez

Basketball

Shooting hoops outside,
Hot sun, beaming on my neck,
Dribbling on the concrete,
Shooting off my fingertips,
Watching it go through the air.

Matthew Carr

Summer

Summer sun shining
Riding my bike down the street,
The wind in my hair
Swerving up and down the street,
Playing outside anytime.

Paige Palmer

Video Games

Video games are
Really fun to play all day,
But not all the time.
You can play them on systems
Like PS2 and Game Cube.

Sean Griggs

Tanka

Football is awesome
It's a brown ball that you use
You can score touchdowns
There are cheerleaders for football
Touchdowns are worth several points.

Joe Zapata

4-Wheeler

Gearing up to ride,
Getting stuck in a mud field,
Driving in the pond,
Driving through the small timber,
Getting cleaned up is dirty.

Seth Haney

Swimming

Swimming is so fun,
Running, running, catch a wave,
Swimming every day,
Making sure you have some fun,
Making sure you don't get hurt.

Summer Heckethorn

Softball Season

Spring and summer sun
Traveling, eating, playing
Pitching, and catching,
Fielding, throwing, and cheering,
Losing, winning, playing hard.

Sydney Burnett

The Moon

The moon shines brightly
Over the wonderful trees
It shows the big world
What it needs to see and love
Which is all the shining stars.

Tiffany Triplet

Gentle Spring

Spring rain falling down
Falling in a gentle mist
Cool and gentle breeze.
As the leaves rustle gently,
We know that spring has arrived.

Cara Johnson

Summer

Summer is awesome,
Swimming, playing, no more school.
The beach, pool, and sand
Are great in the summer time.
It's fun to run in the sun.

Huma Liptak

Ocean Poetry

Our sixth graders at F.M.S. study an oceanography
unit in science where they research and find ten
facts about a living animal or plant from the ocean.
In language arts class, students use their research
facts to create a poem.

Hammer Head Headache

I am the Great Hammerhead Shark,
I have good hearing, even in the dark.

I like to eat rays, squid, crabs, and bony fish,
But rays I like best, they would be my wish.

I can live for up to 30 long years,
During the day, I form schools with my peers.

I dwell worldwide, but I prefer warm and shallow,
I can go up to 260 feet deep, for prey I need to follow.

I can get to 11 and a half feet long,
I'm the biggest specie of hammerhead, I need to be
strong.

I can produce about 13-55 of those hammerhead
babies,
They start out small and that's no maybe.

When I glide along in the water, I swing my head
from side to side,
Since my eyes are at the tips of my "hammers," no
lunch of mine can hide.

Benjamin Boender

The Fatty Seal

Hi! I am the Elephant Seal
My scientific name is Mirounga leonine.
No one knows my size, because I am just
too big and fat.
I can be found along Baja, California, and
Guadalupe Island.
I am the seventh in the food chain.
I eat squid, large fish, and penguins and
I have very few predators.
I can get eaten by my own kind.
I am so big that my heart is 93 pounds,
my skin is 250 pounds, and my blubber is
1,450 pounds.
I am brown and
I have a big nose.
Even though I am a seal, I am not on shore much.
I swim like a regular seal.

Amber Thomas

Don't Step On Me

I am the Crown of Thorns Starfish,
There are thorns all over me.
I can be many different colors,
It hurts to step on me.
You can find me in a coral reef,
Mainly the Great Barrier one,
Crawling all over the ground.
You better watch out for me, I only eat coral,
It doesn't matter which color or kind,
Please, don't step on me!
When I join hands with one of my friends,
I can eat 30% more,
Please don't step on us!

Emily Manning

The Royal Queen Angelfish

I am the Queen Angelfish.
Thankfully, I am my own favorite colors;
Blue, green, and yellow.
I like to eat sponges, algae, hydroids, and bryozoans.
My beautiful castle is in the wonderful
Coral reefs of the tropical Atlantic waters.
I love my servants for feeding me
Parasites at the cleaning stations.
I'm different because, well, I'm a queen!
Of course I am very graceful and slow,
So my servants and peasants can see me.
I have a lifespan of 15 years
And then my daughter will take over.
That's pretty much the life of me!

Jessie Warner

Silent Swimmer

I am a Saw Tooth Eel.

My body is slivery, slivery black,
I am now hungry for a small snack.

I have thin jaws, but very sharp teeth,
I live in the Pacific Ocean 2,000 meters beneath.

I am in the mood for a yummy fish,
Maybe some krill, oh, how I wish.

I am as long as two feet put together,
I must look out for a very large netter.

That would not be good on my delicate structure,
It would hurt as much as acupuncture.

Deep in the ocean, where no sunlight gets through,
There go my predators, the shark, and the whale blue.

I will move down, deeper and dimmer,
That is why I am a silent swimmer.

Matthew Carr

The Speed of Gold Lightning

I am the Sebae Clownfish,
I am small, only 12 centimeters tall.

My poundage is light,
For I am only 1 or 2 pounds.

I eat very small crustaceans,
But the larger ones are what I dread,
Along with the nudibranchs and starfish,
And those very deadly worms.

I'm a very rare little fish,
So small and not tall.

I only live in a small place
Called the Northern Indian Ocean.

In the anemones is where I roam,
For that is where I call home.

I live there for one reason,
And one reason only,
No other fish may go where I live,
For they will die of shock.

Only I may enter my home.

I am black and gold,
Until I grow old,
Where I turn brown as dirt.

I swim away for which I may,
Make a new home every month.

I am as fast as lightning,
Swimming through the coral blue.

I must make a great life for me,
As I only live 46 months.

Sara Adam

Ferocious Fishy

I am Sam, the killer whale,
I look kind of like a dolphin.

Where I live is in deep and shallow waters,
And I am usually within 500 miles of land.

What I eat is stuff like fish, birds,
Turtles, seals, and a lot of other things.

I eat on an average of 500 pounds a day,
My speed is about 35 miles per hour.

I move like a dolphin, or a great white shark.
I move with my fins stuck out.

Seth Simmons

Limerick (lim'er-ik) Poetry

A humorous, five-lined poem with an a-a-b-b-a rhythm & rhyme, using one couplet and one triplet.

Pink Fleece in Greece

There once was a woman in Greece
Who could not stop wearing pink fleece,
Because of an elf
That bewitched herself
A gift from her six- year-old niece.

Dharmini Guanel

A Limerick

Catcher, catcher, you're the one
Catcher, catcher, face that sun
Chase that ball
Do not fall
Catcher, catcher, we just won!

Erica Topping

A Mouse Named Larry

There once was a mouse named Larry.
He had too much to carry.
Though he was strong
He was really wrong
To stop and try to grab that berry.

Hanna Greiner

Popper and the Copper

There once was a man named Popper
He was hiding from the copper
He hid in an alley
With his cat, Meowy
Popper doesn't like all the coppers.

Mason Ellis

Meg

There once was a girl named Meg,
Who played a pirate named Peg,
She was a good actor
So I said, "hi" as I passed her
And I wished her to break a leg.

Sara Adam

My Grandma

My grandma broke her hip
If only she didn't slip.
I hope she gets better
Because I love her,
Man, she went for a trip!

Dylan Gridley

Pasture Poems
Inspired By Robert Frost

Famous American poet, Robert Frost, (1874 -1963), author of "The Pasture," inspired us when we read his old-fashioned poem. The following poems, written by our sixth graders, are updated interpretations of Frost's "Pasture" poem.

The Pasture

I'm going out to clean the pasture spring;
I'll only stop to rake the leaves away
(And wait to watch the water clear, I may):
I shan't be gone long.—You come too.

I'm going out to fetch the little calf
That's standing by the mother. It's so young,
It totters when she licks it with her tongue.
I shan't be gone long.—You come too.

Robert Frost

Pasture Poem

I'm going out to play basketball:
Alley-oop it to Vincent, drive to the lane
Watch it drop through the hoop, just like it's rain
I shan't be gone long. —You come too.

I'm going out to hang with my friends:
Watch a movie, or go to the mall
When we're walking around, we'll be sure not to fall
I shan't be gone long.—You come too.

Joseph Hietpas

Pasture Poem

I'm going out to rule the world
I'm sure I'll be amazing,
It's me they'll be craving
I shan't be gone long. —You come too.

Dorian Larson

Couplets

A two-lined, often humorous poem
that ends in rhyme.

My Couplets

I love to go outside and be in the sun
To swim, jump, play, and run, it's loads of fun.

I walked into the county fair.
I saw a clown with green hair.

I looked at the flag they call Old Glory.
It reminded me of an old war story.

When everyone finally sat in their place,
That's when we took time to say grace.

The coach recommended me to play basketball.
Maybe the reason was I was eight feet tall.

Cheyanne Laux

Holiday & Winter
Poetry

Christmas Thoughts

Christmas is coming closer,
The snow is growing deep.
The tree that we had planted,
Is full of tinsel and leaves.
The presents are so big,
The pickle yet not found.
The smell of apple cider,
Lingers all around.
The stockings were hung,
On the mantel with care.
As we drift off to sleep,
A thought in a mind.
We will have great fun tomorrow,
With snow divine.

Sesali Martin

Christmas

Christmas
I see presents
I smell hot apple cider
I hear snowplows running through the streets
I taste warm chewy treats
I touch soft, cold snow
Christmas

Chris Font

Winter Poem

Snow tracks on the floor
People in the Christmas store.

All through the night
Oh, what a sight.

To be in a winter wonderland
We can decorate the tree.

Oh, let our spirits be free, oh joy,
When we find that one special toy.

We all sit around,
And there is no sound.

When we gather to pray,
About that wonderful day.

Now it is night,
When we get tucked in tight.

All through the night,
The sound is down and the lights turn out,

That's the end of tonight.

Hailey Lathrop

Things Found
Poetry

Things Found in a Locker Room

Showers dripping,
Towels whipping.

Dirty towels in a bin,
People file in.

Clothing on the floor,
Slamming locker doors.

Here we go for gym class,
The bell rings at last.

Lockers in a row,
Man, who's got B.O.?

THE WONDERFUL BLONDES IN 2ND HOUR:

Makayla Kessel
Hanna Greiner
Kara Greiner

Things You Find in a Movie Theater

Gum stuck under the chairs,
Sometimes they give great scares

Wrappers all over the floor,
And half-drunken drinks galore

Popcorn popping rapidly,
People laughing happily

Can't see over people's hair,
Especially when the good part is there

Stand in line to get your ticket,
While I go get the Chicklets

Many teens disturbing others,
While little kids are cuddling with their mothers

It is very, very dark,
We are eating candy sharks

The candy stand closes in five,
While the movie is premiering live.

Allison Angstead
Sydney Burnett
McKenna Ledger
Keri Schwarz

Things You Did or Played With When You Were Little

Baby dolls a tiny thing,
Blankets that are soft.

Pillow cases droolificated,
Bottles full of stuff.

Little baby LaLa dolls,
And building things with blocks.

Running around the room all day,
In a diaper, not afraid to go and play.

Playing with the dump-dump trucks,
Little boys and Spiderman,
Little girls and Barbie dolls.

Emily Manning
Sesali Martin
Kayla Weirup

Miscellaneous
Poetry

Sesali

Sesali is her name!
We call her Sesie,
She is very messy.
She will never lie,
But sometimes she tries to fly.
She doesn't eat candy a lot,
And she doesn't have a blood clot.
She likes sheep,
She always says a peep.
Sesali is her name!

Kayla Weirup

Danielle

Danielle is sweet,
She sometimes eats.
I've never seen her fight,
Except during the night.
We call her Dannie,
But never Lannie.
She has one brother,
And definitely a mother.
She doesn't like school,
I think she is cool!

Kayla Weirup

The Year 2008

Two-zero-zero-eight,
A time to start anew,
A place for me and you;
Two thousand and eight, 2008.

School's still in session,
Pencils, books and bags,
Over-achievers and lags;
Two thousand and eight, 2008.

Soon summer will come,
People going their separate ways,
Some counting the days;
Two thousand and eight, 2008.

Two-zero-zero eight,
A time to start anew,
A time and place for me and you;
Two thousand and eight, 2008.

Makayla Ann Kessel

A Day in the Life of a Lion

He waits in the brush
Patiently, he sits
Waiting, waiting
For just the right moment
Then it comes
Quickly he leaps
Out of the brush
Then he lands
On top of
His little Sister

They tumble
And play
Rolling in the grass
Soon
They get tired
And slowly
Very slowly

They plod away
To their home in the tall grass
To where Mother
And Father lounge
They fall asleep
Awaiting tomorrow's
Adventure.

Taalia Larson

STORIES By

6th Grade Students of

The Fairfield Middle
School

2008

Gone Crazy

Samantha had owned Poodle and Cinnamon, her two dogs, ever since she was a little girl. Samantha's dog, Poodle, was a good dog since birth, along with his sister, Cinnamon. Cinnamon looked almost exactly like Poodle, except for a white spot under her right ear. Poodle and Cinnamon lived with Samantha and her parents, George and Barbra, and Samantha expected them to for the rest of their lives. Until that one day in the park.

One day Samantha, Poodle, and Cinnamon went to the park. Although Poodle was acting grumpy, they went anyway. When they got to the park, Samantha decided to play fetch. Samantha threw the ball and Poodle and Cinnamon would go fetch it, but then they didn't come back.

"Poodle! Cinnamon!" Samantha screamed over and over again.

Then she thought she heard whimpering behind the trees. She went over to the trees and saw nothing. Then Samantha wondered if they might have gone home. She decided to go home and look for them. When she got to her house, the door was already open. She saw some red liquid dripping on the ground. The dripping had lead to the upstairs bathroom.

At this point, Samantha was so scared she was

starting to cry. When she got to the top of the stairs, she turned to the right and saw no one in the bathroom but a pitcher of juice knocked over on the floor. Samantha stopped crying, dried her tears, and began to clean up the juice.

She ran down to the kitchen to get a washcloth. When she got to the sink, she heard knocking at the door. Samantha ran to the door, still a little scared. When she opened the door, no one was there. She looked down and saw Poodle's and Cinnamon's collars drenched in blood. There was also a note that said, "If you want to see the remaining of your two dogs, I suggest you stop running away from me."

Samantha didn't understand. She wasn't running away from anyone. She was just trying to find her dogs. Then she started freaking out! Where was Cinnamon and Poodle? What did this person want from her? The questions kept running through her mind as she stood alone at the door, but then she got the feeling she wasn't alone. Someone started breathing down her neck. She felt a hand on her right shoulder. She was definitely not alone.

Samantha woke up. She looked around the room and saw white walls. They weren't only white; they were cushioned walls, too. Samantha tried to move, but her straitjacket wouldn't let her.

Samantha never lost her dogs Cinnamon and Poodle. In fact, she never had dogs named Cinnamon and Poodle or parents named George and Barbra. She was just one of the Help for the Helpless Center's patients. She was crazy.

Lalita Martin

The Harp

Chapter One

It is said that on the full moon, there is a beautiful maiden with the tail of a fish, who will rise out of the river and softly play a harp on the bank. No one has ever seen this maiden, but many have claimed to hear the soft strumming of the harp. However, when they find the source of the music, all they see is a strange harp sitting on the side of the river. This is where Rhasha's story begins.

"Hurry up! Hurry up!" Mary yelled excitedly. "We're going to Grandpa's house today!"

"I know, I know," Rhasha said back. He wasn't too excited about going to Grandpa's house. Even though Grandpa told good stories, and Grandma made a mean cherry pie, there wasn't much to do. Rhasha couldn't understand why his little sister, Mary, loved it there so much.

"Come on!" Mary yelled again.

"All right, all right already. Let's tell Mom and Dad, and then we will go," Rhasha replied. So off they went. When they got to the house, nobody was home, so Rhasha decided to go exploring. Their grandparents lived right by the woods, and there was a river in the woods, so it was great for exploring. "You coming?" Rhasha asked Mary.

"No," Mary replied, "I'm staying here with Mud." Mud was the family dog. They had found him wandering around their front yard one day. They had put up signs, but nobody claimed him. Mary loved him so much, and she begged their parents so much, that they had to keep him.

"Well, I'll be back in a half hour or so. If Grandpa or Grandma come home, tell them I'm exploring," Rhasha explained.

"Umm, o.k.," Mary replied. "Bye."

"Bye."

Rhasha was quite familiar with the forest by now, and there was one tall tree that was great for climbing. It was right by the river, so it had a beautiful view. As Rhasha got to the third branch and looked out, he saw something he had never noticed before. A harp was sitting on the bank of the river. Rhasha climbed down, walked up to the harp, and tried to play it, but it wouldn't make a sound. Then he tried to move it, but it didn't budge. All of a sudden Rhasha heard his name being called.

"Rhasha, lunch time!" It was his little sister, Mary.

"Coming!" Rhasha yelled back.

* * * *

"Grandpa," Rhasha said later at lunch, "have you ever seen a harp by the river before?"

"Ahh, you finally saw that," his grandpa replied. "Well, legend says that on the full moon, a maiden with the tail of a fish…"

"You mean a mermaid!?" Mary interrupted.

"Yes, a mermaid," Grandpa continued, "will come out of the river and play the harp. Many have claimed to hear the music, but none have ever seen this mermaid."

126

"A mermaid? Oh, please," Rhasha said in disbelief, "everyone knows they aren't real, I mean, come on."

"Suit yourself," Grandpa sighed, "but tonight's the full moon."

* * * *

"Come here Mud," Rhasha whispered. He was going to see if this legend was real or not. "Come on, good boy. Now let's go."

At first when Rhasha got to the river, he didn't know what to do, so he hid behind a big rock. What seemed like hours went by, and Rhasha was getting ready to give up and go home. Then suddenly, the air got a light, crisp feel, like something magical was happening. SPLASH! Something had leaped out of the water. Then he heard the noise; a harp, softly playing. Rhasha stood up and looked in the direction of the harp. A silhouette, of what looked like... the mermaid! Mud started to bark like crazy.

"Shut up, you dumb dog!" Rhasha yelled angrily. When he looked back, the mermaid was gone. He was mad at Mud for scaring the mermaid off, but at the same time, he was filled with awe. So *it's true,* he thought, *it's really true.*

Scales

Chapter Two

"Hello? Anybody home?" Rhasha felt something prod his head.

"Come on! Wake up or I'll jump on you!" Rhasha opened his eyes to see his sister flying toward him. Before he could move, she landed right on his stomach.

"Ouch! Mary, what do you want?"

"Mom said that it's time for breakfast," she replied.

"Is that it?" Rhasha groaned.

"No," Mary paused, "she also said that you have to do whatever I tell you to."

"She did not say that!" Rhasha replied. He was getting annoyed.

"Yes, she did."

"Did not!"

"Oh, fine," Mary admitted, "but the breakfast part was true."

* * * *

Later that day Rhasha and Mary were playing hide-and-seek.

"Do I have to play, Mary?" Rhasha complained.

"Yes, you do… please?" she said, staring at him with wide eyes.

"All right, I'll play, but don't make that face. I'll be it.

And remember," he called after her, "twenty seconds is all you get!"

He turned around to face a tree. "Here goes, one… two… three…"

Mary had run to the forest where they had first seen the harp. It was still there, but it would disappear from time to time. Also, no matter how hard Rhasha and Mary looked, they could never find the mermaid. "Eighteen…nineteen…twenty! Ready or not, here I come!"

The ground was squishy and wet because of all the rain they'd been getting. Mary had left deep footprints that Rhasha could easily follow. First, they led to the woods. They led past the harp and then disappeared at the climbing tree. Rhasha was going to look up in the tree, but got distracted. He thought he saw something glint in the light. He walked over to a bush where he thought he saw the light. When he looked into it, all he saw were two muddy stones. *Oh well,* he thought as he started to leave. Then he saw it flash again. This time he was sure it was coming from the rocks. He grabbed them and turned around to go to the river when suddenly, something landed with a thud on his back.

"Ahhhhhhh!" Rhasha shouted as he fell. Once the thing got off of his back, he quickly got up and whipped around to face his attacker. It was…Mary.

"Scared you, didn't I!" she said. "You should have seen the look on your face!"

"What are you trying to do, kill me?!" Rhasha said angrily. Mary ignored him and started to laugh. Rhasha picked up the stones and headed for the river again. Mary stopped laughing.

"Where are you going?" she asked.

"Somewhere," Rhasha replied, still angry. He bent down to wash the rocks in the river, but to his surprise, they did not turn grey when he took them out of the water. They glowed an eerie green. They were smooth and flat, but had an odd-looking point at one end. They shone brightly.

Mary stood behind him with a look of disgust on her face.

"Ewww, what are those?" she groaned.

"I honestly don't know," he replied. Then it hit him, "But I bet Grandpa would!"

* * * *

"Oh," Grandpa said, "these are scales."

"Scales," Rhasha questioned, "like on a fish?"

"Not exactly–"Grandpa started to say.

"Not a fish!" interrupted Mary. "A mermaid! She's back! The mermaid is back!"

"Sorry to disappoint you, but it's not a mermaid, either," Grandpa sighed. "These are dragon scales."

"A dragon?! That's impossible!" Rhasha stuttered.

"Is there a legend about a dragon, too?" Mary asked. She was now bouncing in her seat.

"I can't help you there," Grandpa replied. "But if you're going to go look for it, I'd suggest the cave by your climbing tree."

Before Rhasha could do anything, Mary had shot out the door. Rhasha looked outside.

"Well, what are you waiting for?" Mary shouted. "Let's go!"

* * * *

"Are we there yet?" groaned Mary.

Rhasha sighed, "If you're going to complain the whole time, why did you come in the first place?"

They got to the river and went past the climbing tree to where Rhasha had first found the scales.

"I don't see anything," Mary complained.

"Well, we will have to look around a bit," replied Rhasha. They searched until Mary found a cave. It was almost totally hidden by moss and plants.

"You think this is it?" asked Mary.

"Only one way to find out…"

They walked into the cave and were immediately swallowed by blackness. Rhasha took the flashlight they had brought with them and flipped it on. They both froze. Lying there in the middle of the cave was an enormous dragon. Nothing moved. At first all they could do was stare. Then Mary started to scream.

"Shhh!" Rhasha whispered. "You don't want to wake it up, do you?"

It didn't move. Rhasha went outside the cave and returned a moment later with some rocks and a long stick.

"You aren't going to throw those at it are you?" Mary asked nervously.

All Rhasha answered was, "Be prepared to run at any minute."

First he gently tossed a rock near the dragon's head. Nothing. Then he threw another, only harder. Still nothing. He threw a large rock and it hit its belly. Silence.

"Why isn't it doing anything?" Mary asked.

"I don't know," Rhasha replied.

"Is it dead?"

"I don't know."

"Throw a rock at its head."

Rhasha picked up a small stone and threw it. It hit the dragon's head with a thud, but still nothing happened. Then he grabbed the stick and walked very carefully toward the dragon.

"Is it breathing?" whispered Mary.

Rhasha took the stick and opened its mouth. He glanced down at its belly, but it wasn't moving.

"I don't think so," Rhasha decided. "It must be dead."

Mary and Rhasha started to explore the cave, being very careful just in case the dragon woke up.

"Mary," Rhasha said suddenly, "come here."

"What?" Mary asked, coming over to Rhasha.

"Look."

There, nestled in with the rocks was a single pearly white egg. It trembled and twitched. Then it cracked, and a piece fell out…

Taalia Larson

Mr. Linden's Library

Mary was a girl of adventure. She loved to read and make stories of her own. One day, Mary walked into Mr. Linden's Library toward the restricted section. Mary loved walking through this section of the library just to look at the odd names of the books. Mary stumbled. As she got up from the ground, she noticed she had tripped over a book. This book had a blank cover, and although it was lying in the middle of the aisle, it was covered in a thick layer of dust.

Mary tried to pick up the book, but as if it were glued to the floor, the book would not budge. All of a sudden, a strong wind came from a window nearby and flung the cover of the book open with spectacular force. The pages of the book turned and turned in the power of the breeze. Mary noticed that the pages were completely blank. Finally the pages stopped turning. Right before Mary's eyes, a sentence appeared on the blank page. The sentence read, "Evil lies within these pages."

Then an unknown force slammed the book shut. Mary jumped at the sound of footsteps coming toward her. She turned around just in time to see Mr. Linden coming around the corner.

"Hello, Miss Mary," he said. "What brings you to the restricted section today?"

"Oh, um, just looking," Mary replied.

"Ah, I see. And have you found anything?"

Mary couldn't resist. She just had to ask about the book she had found.

"Yes, actually, and I would like to ask you about it," she said. Mary stepped aside to reveal the book. Mr. Linden's face went pale. He gulped.

"I see. Miss Mary, it appears you have found the worst of all the books in this library. Evil lies within its pages."

"Mr. Linden, may I ask why on earth you are keeping it in the library?"

"Well, I've tried to get rid of it, but somehow it keeps coming back. Please, Miss Mary, do not let curiosity carry you."

And he was gone.

Mary could not help herself. The book was too tempting! She stuck the book inside her bag and left.

That night Mary lay awake, flipping through the pages of the book. She pondered and pondered over how something so simple could be so dangerous. Mary tried, but could not keep her eyes open. Before long, she drifted off to sleep, leaving the book open. Through the night, a vine began to grow out of the book. It grew and grew until it covered everything in sight…including Mary. Mr. Linden had warned her, but now it was too late.

Brooke Stever

The Seven Chairs

Bob was a regular kid. It was a regular spring day. He was off to do his daily chores, until he saw it. No one else saw it. He saw a nun flying in a chair. He saw her for a second, but then she disappeared into the clouds.

Bob ran off to tell his boss, Mr. Krumple. Bob worked at a barn for Mr. Krumple. "Mr. Krumple! I just saw a nun flying in a chair!"

Mr. Krumple didn't look the least bit interested.

"Maybe she was in a hurry," said Mr. Krumple, without looking up from his work. Bob walked away, disappointed.

In the next week, Bob saw five more flying chairs, each with a different person. Each time he tried to tell Mr. Krumple, he didn't listen. Bob decided he would follow the next chair.

The next day, Bob saw another chair. The person in it looked familiar, but he didn't care. He ran after it. It led him to a huge palace with stained glass windows and gigantic doors. He slowly pushed one open and walked in.

He went through long corridors, great halls, and just about everything else. He was about to give up, when he heard a familiar voice.

"Ah, all six of you are here. So here is my plan. No

one knows we are here, except my pesky worker, Bob. He may be nearby. We might have to kill him."

Then Bob realized who the person in the seventh chair was. It was Mr. Krumple.

Bob tried to stay hidden so he could hear more. Who were these people? What were they doing? Mr. Krumple kept talking.

"Now with our awesome take-over-the-world-machine, we can, well, take over the world. These flying chairs are essential to the plan. We'll be able to stay hidden."

Bob took all this in. They were going to take over the world and kill him. Bob decided he'd heard enough. There was only one thing to do. He pulled Super Teddy Bear from his pocket. He decided Super Teddy should use his laser eye. So Bob jumped out from behind a wall and yelled, "Super Teddy Laser Eye, activate!" All seven of them fell down dead. *Wow*, thought Bob. *That was easy*. But then Super Teddy started shaking. Bob knew what was happening. He read it in the instruction manual. Super Teddy was going to blow up. Bob tossed Super Teddy and ran. Then, the castle blew up. Bob ran home and bought a new Super Teddy.

Coren Hucke

Saying Good-Bye

Chapter 1

Hi, my name is Katrina F. Cadmus and I'm 15 years old. My initials are K.F.C. Sometimes I wonder if my parents named me after a bunch of chicken legs. And this is my story…

It all started at the dance. Being in 9th grade and a freshman in high school, this was my first high school dance. I was dancing with my friends, and all of the sudden my dad runs into the gymnasium and comes straight to me. I wanted to crawl into a hole and hide there forever. I mean, who wants their dad showing up in the middle of a dance, dressed in over-alls and a t-shirt, smelling like cows? Anyway, I knew this couldn't be good.

"Katrina, you have to come back to the farm," Dad said, hurriedly. He sounded worried.

"Why? What's wrong? Is everyone all right?" I asked.

Dad answered, "It's Chester. He was cutting wood and got too close to the saw. He has a deep cut. Even the doctor's worried."

I nodded my head. We ran outside and got into the truck. The drive home was silent. I was sitting there praying it wasn't serious and that Chester would live. Chester is my younger brother and only 12. My older brother, Henry, is away at college and is 20 years old.

We were nearing the house and we saw the doctor coming down the front steps. Dad stepped on the gas and reached the driveway faster than I thought possible. He turned off the engine and jumped out of the truck and started talking to him. I watched and slowly opened my door and got out of the front seat. The doctor shook his head and Dad hung his, and I knew; Chester was dead.

I stopped dead in my tracks. It can't be. Not yet. No, he couldn't be dead. Not Chester. Oh, this can't be, no, not to him, not to me! I just stood there for I don't know how long. Tears took over my eyes as I stared helplessly at the ground. Finally, Dad came over and wrapped me into one of his giant bear hugs. I didn't want to have to say good-bye.

School

Chapter Two

Over the next few weeks, our refrigerator filled up fast. We had all the cookies and brownies we could ever want. However, they still didn't take away the emptiness inside my stomach. It was as if someone had just reached inside of me and took out my insides. I don't remember those last few weeks very well. It was as if the whole world had stopped. Henry had come back from college and was staying in his old bedroom.

Chester's funeral was about a week after the accident. I still remember that cold October morning, blowing on my face as I watched the coffin being loaded into the back of that long black car.

I didn't go to school for a while. And when I did go back, people wouldn't quit asking me about what had happened. I was the biggest talk of the school for the next two weeks, but no big surprise there. I mean, when someone dies, everybody wants to know everything.

How Do You Live Without
Someone You Love?

Chapter Three

"How are you doing?" asked Henry.

"Fine, you?" I asked back. He sat next to me on the back steps that looked over the garden.

"OK. I still can't believe he's gone. It feels as if he's still here, just hiding so no one can find him," he answered.

I looked at him. Deep down I knew I felt the same way. No matter how hard I tried, I just couldn't forget that feeling; the feeling that he was just upstairs in his room or hiding away in the garden. But I also knew, he was gone.

I looked at Henry and asked, "How do you live without someone you love? When someone you loved so dearly just vanishes and no matter how hard you try, you can't forget them; or for that matter, remember everything you had known about them?"

"Katrina, sometimes I swear that you're older than me when you speak like that. As for your questions, I really don't know. Sometimes I catch myself thinking the same thing," Henry said.

"What are you two doing out here?" a voice asked.

I turned around and saw Aunt Vera. Let me tell you about Aunt Vera. She was my favorite aunt and still is to this day. Aunt Vera loved nature and was always outside. She lived a mile or two up the road with Uncle Richard, who equally loved the outdoors. Vera was mom's older sister and loved children, but never could have any of her own. So we were like her adopted children and she was the coolest aunt anyone could ever have. She always seemed to know exactly what you needed or wanted.

"We were just talking," answered Henry.

"About what, may I ask?"

"Stuff," I replied.

"Oh, ok, I get it. I'll just go help your mom with lunch," Aunt Vera informed us. We watched her go into the house where all the delicious smells were coming from.

"Well," said Henry," I think I'm going to see what they're cooking and taste it for them, just to make sure it's ok."

I laughed, "You go ahead."

With that, he turned to go inside. I looked up at the sky. The clouds looked light and fluffy as they effortlessly drifted past. I wondered if Chester was up there now, lying on a cloud watching me. I wondered if he was happy, or if he missed us, just as much as we missed him? I wondered if he still thought about me, or if he had already forgotten me? How would I ever know? Will I ever know?

Hanna Greiner

Falling

One day, I went out to the barn with Jessie. We saddled Hampton and Tia. This was going to be a great day for a long trail ride. Jessie and I were talking and laughing. We got up the hill and started trotting. We took the long way to the field because we had lots of time.

I could tell Hampton wanted to run, so when we got to the field, I let him loose. He happily broke into a canter. Tia and Jessie and Hampton and I both cantered for about ten minutes. As we were walking them out, we were still talking and laughing. We decided that we were going to canter again. I wish I had never decided that. We started cantering and it turned into a gallop. We were side by side. All of a sudden, Hampton turned and I slid off the other way. I was falling and falling. The world seemed to slow down as I fell. All of a sudden, right as I was about to hit the ground, it sped back up and I tried to stop myself. Hampton kept going without me.

Jessie got off Tia and asked, "Huma, are you all right?"

"I don't think so," I said.

She ran and got Hampton and I tried to mount. I couldn't. She ran and got Tia and rode back to her mom. I started walking back, leading Hampton.

When I got back, Shane, Jessie's mom, and my riding

teacher called my dad and took me home. I had not even started crying yet, so Shane seemed to think it was just a sprain. We got home and Shane and Jessie left. I talked to my dad and started crying. He took me to the doctor. I got an x-ray and I got a brace for my wrist.

A couple of days later, I got my first-ever cast. It was pink.

Now it is off, but I haven't been riding much.

Huma Liptak

Runaway

Chapter One

One hot summer day in Oklahoma, there was a girl named Loretta Garrison cleaning the stalls. She was the child of Luke and Rose Garrison. She was a bright and spirited girl. Her family owned a lot of horses on a stud ranch. The one she liked best was Storm. He was a bay color with a white star on his forehead. He was always so happy to see her, but he was miserable in the stable. He couldn't run very fast with his crippled leg, but Loretta loved him anyway. The other horses didn't like him very much. When she went to take a rest, Storm went up to her.

"Storm, I wish I could just have a little fun here. Swimming in the pond and riding all day! That would make my day," said Loretta.

Storm just wiggled his ears. He liked listening to Loretta. He thought it was interesting just listening to what she had to say.

"I think I'm going to go and eat supper now. Bye, Storm! See you tomorrow!"

That's what Storm was going to do, too. He ate some hay and oats and fell fast asleep. I guess Loretta thought he was really tired when she came in to check. She checked on all of the horses and they were fine. She later went to her room and fell asleep, too.

Chapter Two

The next morning, Storm went to see the other horses in the pasture. One stallion was named Rocket, and he wasn't the nicest, but Storm always tried to be nice. Rocket was a spotted appaloosa that was white and brown.

"What are you looking at, crippled leg?" mocked Rocket.

"Nothing at all, I just want to join you guys."

"Well, you can't because you can't run as fast as us!" said Rocket.

Storm felt left out. He always did, even when he didn't have his crippled leg. They treated him like a pile of dirt. That's when he decided to run away.

Chapter 3

He decided to break open the gate when all of the horses were sleeping. When he did, there was a big, "POW!!" but none of the horses woke up. He galloped and galloped, till he found a safe place to sleep. He found a meadow with a natural lake, and decided to sleep there for the night.

Chapter 4

"Shhhh…..be quiet! He is waking up!"

"Ahhhhhhh!!!" Storm screamed.

He was surrounded by a wild herd of horses! He didn't know whether to run, or to stay in his place.

"Hi. I'm Melody. I am the leader of this herd. Glad to meet you. What is wrong with your leg?"

"Um…..it's kind of crippled. I was running with the other horses, and I tripped. I fell to the ground, and there you go. I'm crippled," said Storm.

"What other horses?" asked Melody.

"Well, the other horses at the stud ranch. They aren't that friendly. It's all because of this leg. And I ran away."

"Oh. Well, here we include any horse, even with a crippled leg. Do…uh…do you want to live with us? You will never be alone at all," insisted Melody.

Storm had to think a little. He didn't know where to go and these horses were friendly. They were a lot nicer than the other horses, and Storm felt a little spark around Melody.

Chapter 5

"Yes. I will join, if that is ok. I hope it is," Storm replied.

"Great! We were just moving north. Oh, and I bet you want to meet the others, too."

Melody pointed to all of the horses. There were fourteen of them. Some were mustangs, and some were different kinds.

"Hi! My name is Starburst!" she said sweetly.

"Hello. I'm Crystal."

"Nice to meet you! I'm Thunder. Nice to have another horse around."

"I hope you like it here. Name's Lightning. Thunder is my twin," said Lightning.

"Well, good for you, Lightning. Hi, I am Kiwi. I am the youngest. It's soooooo exciting to have a new horse around!!!" expressed Kiwi.

"Well, there are fourteen in our herd, but we can wait to meet the others," joined in Melody.

Jessie Warner

My Personal Experience to Texas

We got set up for our trip to Texas by planning over the phone. My mom, dad, and I went together. We got on a plane and left. I loved the plane ride, but, for my first time on a plane, I didn't want to sit by the window. It took two planes to get to Texas.

Once we got to Texas, my grandma and grandpa were there. They were waiting for us to get to the very busy airport. My grandma and grandpa took us to their house and we slept till morning.

When we woke up, we went to two places in one day. The two places were Padre Island and Mexico. We had a great day. Padre Island was extremely beautiful. Mexico, on the other hand, wasn't so pretty, but I had a good time any-way!

The next day, we went to the River Walk and it was beautiful! It was the most amazing place I had ever been to. The following day it was Easter and my grandma and grandpa got me Easter presents.

Finally, we had to leave and it took two planes back. I will always remember the great time in Texas!!

Leah Browning

Destiny Hope

It had been a year since Zailey died. Zoey just didn't know what to do. She still felt so empty inside. Zoey hadn't changed much on the outside, but on the inside she felt like the world had turned inside of her. Zoey missed Zailey so much! She tried hard not to cry when she thought of her.

It was now the year 2008. Zoey still hadn't made a New Year's resolution, even though it was August and school would be starting up again.

Suddenly, Zoey had a flashback of the past year, of all the people who said they were sorry about Zailey, and knew how Zoey felt. Well, no, they didn't know. Zoey just wished they leave her alone!

When school started up again, Zoey felt a dull thud in her stomach. She had no one to call and see what classes they had together. Tears were welling up in Zoey's eyes, when she heard her name being called. She turned to see it was the guidance counselor, Ms. James. Zoey walked over and found Ms. James and another girl whom she didn't recognize.

"Zoey, this is Destiny Hope. She's new here. I was wondering if you could help her find her way around school," Ms. James finished with a bright smile.

Zoey wasn't sure. She didn't know if she wanted to show around another new kid. Zailey had been the new girl when Zoey first met her.

As if Ms. James sensed her feelings, she quickly said, "Please, Zoey!"

Finally Zoey said, "Oh, all right, I'll do it!"

So, the next day, Zoey met up with Destiny Hope and they compared their classes. As it turned out, they had all of the same classes, and even their lockers were next to each other. Zoey thought that Ms. James had something to do with it.

"Um," Destiny interrupted Zoey's train of thought, "Zoey, I was just wondering if…you would like to come to my house after school?"

"Ok! Why not?" Zoey wasn't sure why she was so excited. She guessed it was because it had been awhile since she had hung around with Zailey, and Destiny Hope reminded her so much of her. Suddenly, Zoey wanted to know more about Destiny Hope!

Where was she from? Is Hope her middle name? Before Zoey knew it, she was feeling attached to Destiny in a way she hadn't felt about anyone since Zailey's death. Over the next few weeks, Zoey and Destiny became very close. With Destiny's help, Zoey was able to get over Zailey's death.

One day as Zoey and Destiny were sitting on Destiny's bed, Zoey finally got the courage to ask the question she so desperately wanted to know.

Zoey asked, "Destiny?"

"Yes?" Destiny answered.

"Well, you know your name, Destiny Hope? Well, is Hope your middle name?" Zoey finished quickly.

"Yes, my daddy always said that I was named Destiny Hope because my destiny was to bring hope," she finished simply.

It was at that moment that Zoey realized that Destiny's name was true. Her destiny was to bring hope and that is what she did! Destiny Hope brought Zoey hope, and for that she was thankful. Zoey was finally able to let go of Zailey's death and live her life with hope and to forever be friends with the girl whose destiny was to bring hope.

Makayla Kessel

Montal

My name is Montal, son of Liral. My dad is Sam. I was born in the castle. I am now 11, and here is my story.

I woke up to a lot of loud explosions. I looked outside and it was just Dad and Grandpa Touchstone training. I went to the fair to cheat out some gambling booths. I got to the fair and saw a new game.

Get a paper net and try to catch a fish. If you catch a fish with a small net, you get ten gold. If you won with the medium net, you get seven gold, and if you use the big net, you would get two gold, I read.

"Ok," I said, "let's win some money!"

I started to play, but it was hard. I started to use magic, but then I lost it all! I didn't know how that had happened, until I looked at the vendor. The vendor was a guard at the castle.

I went to cheat those games that you drop the ball into the box full of pegs. The vendor said I was lucky, but I knew how I kept winning.

A man in a dark hood came to me and asked me if I could show him to the woods. I thought about it. If I needed to, I could blow him to bits.

I said, "That's no problem for me."

We started off and we came to a hotel. He asked if we could stop and pick up some boxes at his hotel. When we got there, he told me what boxes to grab. I turned around to ask him where to take them. Then I saw the necromancer weapons! He was going to kill me!!!

I hit him with a flaming dart. It gave me enough time to get away.

I ran to the castle and yelled to Dad, "Someone just tried to kill me, and it's a necromancer!"

Dad gasped and asked me where he was. Right as he finished talking, we heard a guard say he caught a necromancer. We took him to the castle to question him. The necromancer said that he did it for money. He said that whoever brought the king's crown covered in blood would get fifty million dollars.

Michael Brush

Under The Rug

There once was a house on 34th Street. The owner's name was Harold McGregor. In 1972, Harold was found dead in his study. His body was hidden under a rug and pieces of chair were scattered all over the floor.

In 1980, a man named Curtis Oswald bought the house, but was never heard from again. Some say he was thrown into shock and died when a lump the shape of a man appeared from under the rug. Many men checked, but all that was found were old man McGregor's glasses.

Five years passed and old man McGregor's house fell into the hands of Charles McGregor. One night Charles was sitting in his study, and a lump the shape of a man rose up from the floor and under the rug. Charles got up and ran from the room, only to be knocked unconscious when the door slammed shut in his face. Charles woke up at 10:17 to find no sign of the lump.

Two weeks passed and it happened again. This time Charles took the chair and bashed it over the lump. A terrible groan and then a man's screaming shook the house. Then the lump vanished. He lifted up the rug to reveal the stains from the night old man McGregor died.

Time passed and nothing happened. One night

Charles was getting ready to go to bed when he heard a terrible moan, and thumping noises coming from downstairs. Charles grabbed his gun and ran down the stairs.

As he approached his study, a rotting hand appeared from the kitchen. Charles immediately shot at it and it fell to the floor. The next thing he knew, he was on his back, staring up into his grandfather's rotting face. Harold dragged him to the cellar where a terrible scream was heard from all over town.

A group of people ran to Charles's house and found nothing but a rotting hand, and Charles McGregor hidden under the rug in the cellar. Many say Charles was beaten by the chair in his study, just like his grandfather.

Landon Gamrath

Bob and Frank's Day

"So how's your day today?" asked Bob, as he saw Frank walk into the ice cream store.

"Very interesting," Frank explained.

"How?" Bob asked, with ice cream in his mouth.

"Oh, I wasn't talking to you. I was talking about the super deluxe 12 scoop banana split ice cream extreme with hot fudge and nuts. It's on sale, and it's now $9.99. I'll take one please," Frank answered.

"Oh," coughed Bob, with his ice cream almost gone.

"My day was super-dooper. I went to see "The Blood and Gore of Superman." It's great. His head gets ripped off, and this guy rips out his guts and organs and all that and eats them. It's the best!" said Frank.

"Sounds like fun," laughed Bob. "But I jumped off the Empire State Building and lived, caught King Kong, ate the world's largest cheeseburger, and ran around the world, all in less then 30 minutes," gloated Bob.

"Wow!" yelled Frank.

"I know, I'm awesome!" rejoiced Bob.

They walked over to their rocket ship. They were going to be the first 40-year-old men in space that still lived with their mothers.

"How is a cardboard box going to get us to the moon?" asked Bob.

"Well, my mommy tells me if you believe, think real hard, close your eyes, have imagination, then you can do anything," replied Frank.

"Oh, like the time I shot your dog because you said it was an alien, or the time we burned down Mrs. Monroe's house, because you said it was the evil bunny castle?" They both went silent, then Bob said, "Works for me, let's go!"

"Wait!" yelled Frank. "We have to get the cheese sandwiches!"

He got them.

"Ok, now we can go," nodded Frank.

So now they're in their spaceship and, as you know, they're 40 and live with their mothers. So what happens as they're about to leave? Of course, Mother. That's what happens.

"Bob, honey, come on inside and help your mommy-wommy make some cookie-wookies."

"Mom, not in front of Frank," Bob spoke just loudly enough so only his mom could hear.

"Don't give me that tone, mister, I am your mother and you will do to as I say if you want to stay up later than 8:00 and watch 'When Nerds Attack' tonight!"

"All right, Mommy," Bob muttered.

"What did you say!?"

"Nothing, Mom!" yelled Bob.

Frank was laughing so hard, he started making bubbles come out his nose. Bob gave him the nerd's eye. Frank calmed down. They made cookies. When they were done, the mail came.

"Wow, my 'Freaks, Geeks, and Nerds' magazine came!" shouted Bob. "The rocket will have to wait till tomorrow."

In the magazine there was a paper to fill out. If you sent it in, you could win a trip for two to The Cool Place. The Cool Place is a place that turned special people like Bob and Frank, into cool people like George Lopez. So they filled it out, sent it in, and one week later they won!

When they got to The Cool Place, the person that makes them cool said, "I've never seen people like you. You've got to be kings of the dorks and the nerds. You two are the king of the norks!" Then he called in FBI to take them away.

When they got home, Bob asked, "Mom, are we dorks, nerds, losers, or freaks?"

"Yes, honey, you two are all those things," she replied. "But in a good way, you're those things. That's why I love you."

"Ok," the boys said. They went downstairs to continue getting dates on the Internet. They almost got an 80-year-old, but then she died.

"Why does your mom love me?" asked Frank.

"I don't know," answered Bob.

Bob's mom had a friend over and she asked, "Do you really love Bob?"

"Of course not, I don't think he could get Barney to say 'I love you' to him." They laughed.

Meanwhile... in the basement, the two boys were talking to a six-year-old that got on her mother's account. They got in an insult contest and of course the six-year-old won.

"Well, at least I know big words like, ALL, and you don't, so ha!" typed Frank.

"I know big words too, like *physician, invisible,* and *nork.* That's what you are," typed the 6-year-old.

"Why does everyone call us norks? It's not physically possible to be such a creature," pointed out Bob.

"I'm not sure. Is it the way we dress?" asked Frank.

They were wearing shoes from the 60's, tall socks, jeans rolled up to the knees, plaid shirts with a pocket filled with pens, big thick glasses taped in the middle, and hair combed to the side.

"Nah," said Bob, "We're too good looking. That's why all the girls run in our presence."

Riley Hammel

The Dark

Are you scared of the dark? I used to think being scared of the dark was stupid, until Friday the 13th of March happened to me. Let me introduce myself… I am Samantha Tedrow. I was at Alyssa Murphy's house for her birthday party. She had a lot of friends over. There were Dorian, Katelynn, Lacee, Alina, Brandi, Allison, Erica, Hailey and me.

We were in Alyssa's room when her mom came in and said, "Whatever you girls do, DON'T go down to the basement or go anywhere NEAR it!"

Alyssa was trying to think of something to do, when I suggested *Truth or Dare*. Everyone dared Alyssa and me to go downstairs.

When we opened the door to go down the stairs, we heard a really scary noise. We just pretty much ignored it and then on with the dare. When we were halfway down, something grabbed Alyssa's leg! Alyssa screamed for help. I kicked the thing that was trying to pull her down through the crack in the stairs. Alyssa wanted to run back upstairs, but I told her that it was a dare and that we should just get it over with.

When Alyssa and I reached the bottom of the stairs, we smelled this awful smell.

"It smells like something died down here," said Alyssa.

We walked a little further and Alyssa and I slid in something wet. When I got my cell phone out of my pocket, I shined the light of my phone on what we had slipped on. Alyssa and I screamed so loudly that the dead could hear us. We were looking right at Alyssa's dad and the family dog, Joey. Dead. Right there on the ground. Alyssa was crying so hard when she got back upstairs.

"What's wrong, sweetie?" Alyssa's mom asked.

"You killer! ou killed them!" screamed Alyssa.

"What are you talking about, dear?"

"You killed Daddy and Joey!"

"I thought it was time for your dad to leave this family."

"What? Why? And, well, never mind…what about Joey? Why did you kill him?

"Oh, that stupid dog wouldn't shut up, so I killed him, too, sweetie."

"Don't call me sweetie! I'm calling the cops!"

"Go right ahead, dear, just see what happens to you…"

Alyssa and I called the cops and all the girls went home except for me. We decided for Alyssa to come to my house and live with me.

I got a phone call about three months after Alyssa's father's death. It was the cops. They asked to talk to Alyssa.

"Is this Alyssa Murphy?"

"Yes it is, what is the problem, officer?"

"I'm sorry, but your mother passed away in jail…"

"When did this happen?" asked Alyssa, kind of happy.

"We think maybe two days ago."

Alyssa dropped the phone. She knew her mother wouldn't leave this world without her. Alyssa was so scared that night that she hid in my closet.

I woke up the next morning and found Alyssa in the closet. Dead. I was heart-broken.

Sara Adam

The Pumpkin Smith

He carved with greasy, orange hands. He was hurried, and he needed to move fast. "Only she can stop it," he said.

Venessa, a 12-year-old girl with blonde hair, slid out of bed. She felt for her slippers, but found something else. She leaned down to see what it was, and fell, her silver necklace clattering, which woke her pet rat. The rat squeaked loudly.

"I'm sorry," she said to her rat, as she leaned down to pick up her necklace. Venessa is very clumsy, unlike her mother. She went to see what the orange object was.

"Why, this is a pumpkin," she said, "and the pumpkin is carved with the same symbol as on my necklace."

She got up, slid the pumpkin under her bed, and got ready for school. She got to school early, and walked into the classroom. From the decorations, she realized today was Halloween.

Venessa was excited and could not wait for the bell to ring. The bell finally rang, and she ran home. She really needed to get a costume together.

When she got home, she ran to her closet. She opened the closet door, and a pumpkin rolled out. The pumpkin was carved with an address. *This is really odd,* she thought to herself. *I should go to this house tonight.*

Finally, the time came, and she left for the mysterious house. She arrived at an old, broken-down mansion, which must have once been very beautiful. She knocked on the front door, and a strange man let her in. He had lots of wrinkles, but his eyes looked like a baby's. They were a crisp blue, and looked kind.

He let her in once he saw her necklace, and said, "I am the pumpkin smith, keeper of Halloween. I need you to close the portal to the underworld. The portal has been opened!" he said. "You must throw your necklace into the portal, or else we could all get killed!"

She did as he said, and followed him to the basement. It was dark and creepy, and it gave her the chills. She saw the portal; the portal looked like a big black hole. She threw her necklace in and the portal vanished. She turned around, and the man had disappeared. She went trick-or-treating, and was very confused. The spooks were trapped again, and Halloween was saved.

Charan Williams

164

The Uninvited Guests

I am an adventurous boy, but I would have never been ready for this. One night I had a friend over named Keith, and we were watching TV in the dark when I heard a knocking.

"I got it."

"Ok."

So I went to the door and checked the peep hole; no one there.

"Hmm."

Then I heard it again. It came from the kitchen.

"Did you see my mom pull in, Keith?" I asked.

"No, why?"

"Hmm."

I walked into the kitchen and checked the garage, nothing. Then I heard it again. This time it came from the basement.

"Keith, come here!"

He ran in.

"What!"

"I heard the knocking down there!"

"Let's go!"

We got some flashlights and went downstairs. Then my light fell on a small door. My heart pounded, I could have sworn I saw the doorknob turn.

"Keith?"

…silence…

"Keith?"

Then I saw his flashlight on the ground.

CREEEEEEK!

The door opened and out popped a little being that was part ram, part wolf, part scorpion, part bat.

"Wha-what are you?" I stammered

The thing hissed some indecipherable words. Then more popped out behind it. I backed into a pile of boxes and reached for a weapon, and my hand fell on a pole. I tugged on it and an avalanche of boxes fell on some of the monsters. I hit one of them with the pole, sending it flying through a window which broke and let sunlight in.

"Gahhhhhhhhhhh!" it shrieked.

I jumped into the light and used the pole to reflect the light into a mirror, onto a disco ball that reflected the light everywhere, sizzling the monsters instantly. Then Keith came down the stairs with a flashlight and some nachos.

"Hey, you found out what that noise was yet?" he asked, as he munched.

"Hey, how'd you get upstairs and why'd you drop your light?"

"Hmm, I don't know…"

"Well, anyway, I got hungry and got some nachos," he said.

"Ooooooo, are those jalapeños and beef?"

"Yep."

When we got back upstairs, we watched TV and ate nachos until the doorbell rang.

"I got it."

"Ok."

When I got to the door, it busted open and a demon walked in.

"Keith, get the axe from the attic!"

"Why?"

"JUST GET IT AND BRING IT HERE!!!"

The monster stepped forward. I grabbed a broom and tripped it, then I ran into the living room and slammed the door shut. Then Keith ran in with the axe and handed it to me.

"Ok, good, now help me barricade the door."

After we got it barricaded, Keith asked, "What's in there!?"

"A demon, look for yourself."

Then he looked out the window in the door.

"Holy moley, you're right!"

"Duh!"

"So what now?"

"Let's research it."

I got on the computer, but the power went out.

"I'll get the generator from the garage."

I ran out into the garage and got the generator and came back.

"This will power the room."

I plugged it in and the power came back on.

"It says only silver will kill it."

167

"Well, this axe is silver."

BAM!!! The door cracked.

"Its weak spots are its head and torso."

"Ok, hide and we'll team up on it. The door busted open and only one word could describe the demon... AXED! So we chilled out until my parents came home and we had to explain why there was a dead demon lying on the couch!

Nick Rich

How a Rainbow Got Its Colors

After a long day at work, Mr. Rain let Mr. Rainbow take over his shift. As he left, he remarked, "Mr. Rainbow, I've noticed that instead of making people happy, all you do is make them miserable."

After Mr. Rain left, Mr. Rainbow pondered what he had said. Suddenly inspiration struck!

"It's this suit. It's not colorful enough!"

So he took his suit home and tie-dyed it. There was a little mishap with the dyes, though. He didn't mix them correctly, and they separated into the colors of the rainbow. When he pulled the suit out, it was striped!

"Oh, dear, the boss isn't going to be happy about this one! What do I do? What do I do? What do I do?" he pondered.

"Oh, well, I must go to work anyway," he sighed.

The next day and put on his newly tie-dyed suit. When he got to work, everyone teased him about his new outfit.

"Hey, Rainbow, looks like you fell into some paint!" they scoffed.

"Rainbow, did I miss the circus coming to town?" they laughed.

But when Rainbow thought about it, he was doing his job. He was making people happy.

Moral: Just because someone looks funny, doesn't mean they can't do their job.

Rachel Biggs

Hamster Wheel

Sparky Sparks was sitting on the couch watching his favorite show, *Hamster Wheel*. It's a game show where you spin the wheel to see what prizes you can win. You can win trips, money, and cars, whatever. But sometimes players land on the dreaded PIT. You get dumped into a pit of goo. For years, Sparky had been trying to get on that show, but nobody would pick him. Finally, that day came.

"Welcome to *Hamster Wheel*," the announcer said. "Today we are going to invite one person and his family to come to New York and play Hamster Wheel. We have randomly selected someone in our jumbler. The envelope, please, and the winner is… Sparky Sparks."

"Yeah," Sparky yelled, "I win!"

Sparky Sparks then called the show to get the information. He was the happiest person on earth.

The next day, Sparky woke up early and got ready for the trip. He got dressed and drove to the airport. You see, Sparky lives in Arizona, so it was a long ways away from New York. On the plane, Sparky slept. He was very tired. He dreamed of the game show and hoped he'd win.

After Sparky landed in New York, he saw a sign that said, "Sparky Sparks." There was a man there that asked, "Are you Sparky?"

"Yes," Sparky replied.

"I'm Lloyd, your limo driver."

Sparky dropped his jaw in awe. He'd never have a limo driver before. Lloyd took Sparky to the hotel. There he had a suite and unlimited room service. He loved it.

The next day Sparky slept in. He ordered breakfast and just took it easy. That evening, Sparky and Lloyd drove to Hamster Wheel Studios. He was so excited he couldn't wait.

At 5:00 the announcer, Chuck Fish, started the show. "Hi, I'm Chuck Fish. Today, Sparky Sparks will be joining us." (The crowd cheers). "Come on out, Sparky." Sparky ran out. "Sparky, how excited are you to be here?"

"Very," Sparky answered.

"Great, now let's get started. Sparky, you'll have to spin the wheel at least one revolution. Ready?"

"You bet!"

"Then let's get started!"

Sparky stepped to the wheel and spun it as hard as he could. It spun round and round and round and finally landed on PIT. Before Sparky could even think, the trap door opened and he was swimming in goo. Sparky was laughing. He had had the time of his life.

Matthew Carr

The Combine Incident

One day my grandpa called up my dad and me and said, "The combine's hydraulic fluid tube broke and I need help getting a new one on."

So my dad and I put on our Carharts and went out to the farm to help. When we got there, the combine was sitting out in the barn lot waiting to be moved to the machine shed to change the tube.

My dad and I got into the combine and started it up. Some people think that school bells are loud. Well, this is at least two times louder than a school bell. The air in the cab is musky and dry, and that doesn't help much, either. And to think some people harvest all night, well, that's just not very fun. These seats are far from comfortable. When my dad and I harvest, I don't even get a seat! We'd be in the field for hours at a time. I'd lie, or sit in a slight gap above the driver's seat.

As we started to do a tight turn to get us out of this spot, we felt the combine start to shift, and my dad was having trouble turning the steering wheel. We had run out of hydraulic fluid! We saw the grader ditch coming and my dad grabbed me. We felt the combine lurch and then, BANG, CRASH, REEK! We heard the ladder bending and breaking.

We found about a two-foot opening that we could barely crawl through. When we were out, we saw the combine completely on its side! We used another tractor to pull it out. We lost a lot of corn. That is something I will always remember.

Vincent Horras

Pooh Bear and the
Squad of Super Evilness

My story is about a snake named Fred who was sent to prison for trying to poison someone….Oh wait, I lied! This story is about Pooh Bear! One afternoon, a clearly delirious Pooh Bear had wandered out of the Hundred Acre Woods and into Sesame Street. Here, he was so rudely taken captive by Elmo. What a mean red fuzz ball! Well, anyway, Elmo locked Pooh Bear in a closet.

Pooh Bear was so hungry he was imagining pots of honey! All of a sudden there was a noise from the back of the closet. The noise was not a noise, it was a voice!

The voice said, "Jeffry, is that you?"

"No, I am Pooh Bear!" Pooh replied.

A figure emerged from the dark. It was a short, pink creature with huge ears! Pooh feared it might be a midget hobo. The midget started to speak…

"Oh, my! My dear friend! I thought you were one of my dust bunny buddies... wait, you remember me, don't you? I am Piglet!"

"Oh, dear, thank goodness! I thought you were a hobo!"

Out of nowhere the door crashed down and standing on the other side was…yes, you know who… it was

T-I-double Guh-RRR...TIGGER!

"Fear not, Pooh, and...um...hobo thing! I have come to save you!"

"I AM NOT A HOBO, I AM AN UNSANITARY CAPTIVE!" screamed Piglet. "My name is Piglet!"

"Oh, um...ok. Then let's get out of here!"

They filed out of the closet headed toward the exit.

They opened the door, and standing on the other side was...

GASP! DUN DUN DUUUNNN! IT WAS ELMO!

"You shall never escape the wrath of my red fuzz!" said Elmo, and then he broke out in song, "La LaLa Laaaaa, Elmo's World!"

"Oh, put a sock in it!"

Then out of nowhere, Piglet jumped on Elmo's back, slammed him into the floor, and put him in a headlock.

The unconscious Elmo laid there while Tigger, Pooh, and Piglet ran toward the border of the Hundred Acre Woods! But for how long would they be safe?

The humiliated Elmo crawled to his computer and turned on his webcam. Sure enough, his master, Barney, was logged on. Elmo told Barney what had happened with Pooh, Piglet, and Tigger.

"YOU LET THE CAPTIVES GET AWAY?! You idiot! Now how am I supposed to take over the Hundred Acre Woods? I was planning on having a ski resort there!" yelled Barney.

"I know, boss! But maybe we could bomb the Hundred Acre Woods. All we'd need is a Hundred Acre bomb!" replied Elmo.

"No, that would be too expensive! I'll just bring my

crew to Sesame Street and we can raid the Hundred Acre Woods," Barney said, with an evil smile.

The next day, Barney arrived with him. He had brought the Purple Teletubby, Dora, Diego, Blue (from Blue's Clue's), and the entire clan of Booh-Bahs! Together they snuck into the Hundred Acre Woods.

Once they arrived, they noticed the residents of the Hundred Acre Woods were having a return party for the captives. Barney was enraged!

"Mr. Boss, sir, shouldn't we have a team name?" asked the Purple Teletubby.

"Yes! Yes, indeed!! We will be called the *Squad of Super Evilness!*" replied Barney.

The Squad of Super Evilness approached the party, which was being held at Rabbit's. Barney rang the doorbell.

"Who is it?" called Rabbit.

"Ummm…The pizza man!" replied Barney.

When Rabbit came to the door, the Squad of Super Evilness attacked. The clan of Booh-Bah's jumped on Pooh. Diego tackled Rabbit. Blue put Piglet in a head-lock. Barney and Elmo each gabbed one of Tigger's arms. And Dora and the Purple Teletubby tied Eeyore to a chair.

Rabbit broke free, grabbed her phone, and locked herself in the bathroom. Here, she called the police. The Squad of Super Evilness was sent to jail, but everyone else lived happily ever after.

Brooke Stever

See 1stWorld Books at:

www.1stWorldPublishing.com

See our classic collection at:

www.1stWorldLibrary.com